MARTIN HONERT

MARTIN

CURATED BY KATHLEEN S. BARTELS AND JEFF WALL

HONERT

VANCOUVER ART GALLERY

FOREWORD

For the past three decades Martin Honert has created astonishingly detailed, sculpted forms to visualize the most elusive of phenomena: childhood memory. His art practice, as he remarked to me during our first conversation in his Düsseldorf studio, is above all concerned with the potency of remembered images. With their dramatic shifts in scale and carefully rendered surfaces, Honert's works offer an uncanny recasting of everyday objects and impressions recalled from his childhood in post-war West Germany.

Honert graduated in 1989 from the Kunstakademie in Düsseldorf—a city renowned for its photographers—and his cohort included Thomas Ruff, Andreas Gursky and Thomas Struth. Perhaps not surprisingly, the photograph—and particularly its role in aiding our recall of the past—is an important influence in his work. But his approach is unique among contemporary artists who take up the theme of memory. Rather than emphasize its shadowy qualities, Honert examines the way an image can become stubbornly lodged in our minds and remain there, frozen, over time. In his sculpture, the surrounding context falls away as forms are distilled and colours sharpened.

Along with family photographs, Honert draws his subject matter from school book illustrations, popular stories of his generation and his own boyhood sketches. His aim, however, is neither to psychoanalyze his past nor nostalgize it. "Childhood is a theme for me not because my childhood was especially eventful, or bad, or good," he has explained. "My childhood was exactly as dull and boring as every other childhood. Childhood is a theme for me because I think it's important to discover what's long past but still in the memory as an image." With deliberate emotional detachment, he simply attempts, as he says, "to save an image before it dies within me."

The results of this process are inspired. In Honert's first large-scale installation *Kinderkreuzzug [Children's Crusade]* (1985–7), for example, the artist draws from a curious story he heard in grade school about a group of 30,000 children from Germany and France who, in the thirteenth century, embarked on a crusade to the Holy Land. Honert's intent was not to illustrate these historic events, but to revive a vivid image that passed before his mind's eye when his instructor described the story in class. He based the freestanding, cast-polyester figures on toy soldiers he once owned, enlarging them to life size while retaining the simplistic modelling and featureless faces of his boyhood toys.

Similarly, the artist's floor sculpture *Feuer [Fire]* (1992) is based on a dictionary illustration he encountered in his youth. Over a period of years Honert translated this image into three-dimensions, first in plaster and later in cast polyester resin, which he then hand painted and lit from within. His challenge in creating *Fire* was to "freeze" the luminous, immaterial and perpetually moving appearance of flames into something fixed and rigid. In this way, *Fire* illustrates how the artist views his work generally: as hermetic, self-referential, three-dimensional paintings.

Perhaps what I find most compelling about Honert's work is the fact that he manifests not just childhood memories in three-dimensional form, but the world experienced from a youngster's point of view. *Riesen [Giants]* (2007) illustrates this well. Standing at over two and a half metres high — the height of the tallest known human — and posed like travellers with rucksacks and a walking stick, these towering figures conjure stories of giants from fairy tales. As we crane our necks upward to marvel at them, our perspective returns to that of a child, with all its curiosity and wonderment. A similar effect — though through opposite means — is achieved by *Schlafsaal, Modell 1:5 [Dormitory, Model 1:5]* (2013), a work completed for our presentation in Vancouver and never before exhibited. In this sculpture Honert reconstructs a miniature version of his former boarding school dormitory in one-fifth scale. Empty of students and eerily illuminated amidst a darkened space, *Dormitory* seems to beckon stories spun by an unbridled imagination.

The Vancouver Art Gallery is honoured to introduce the work of Martin Honert to North American audiences for the first time. This important presentation — and its accompanying catalogue — would not have been possible without the support and contributions of many. I extend my sincerest gratitude to lenders Melva Bucksbaum and Raymond Learsy; Ronald Lauder; Ivan and Herbert Moskowitz; Museum of Contemporary Art, Los Angeles; Musée des beaux-arts de Montréal; Museum für Moderne Kunst, Frankfurt am Main; and the Staatliche Museen zu Berlin, who generously parted with artworks from their collections. We are particularly indebted to Matthew Marks and Matthew Marks Gallery, New York, for their support of this project from its inception, their generous contribution as a lender to the exhibition and to the catalogue's realization. The handsome design of this catalogue is the work of Mark Timmings, who was supported by the Vancouver Art Gallery's photographers Trevor Mills and Rachel Topham. Tom Meighan, Director of Operations, skillfully oversaw the work of the Museum Services division. I also acknowledge Kimberly Phillips, curatorial assistant on this project, for her exemplary skills in coordinating both the exhibition and publication.

My sincere gratitude goes to the Vancouver Art Gallery's Board of Trustees for their steadfast commitment to the Gallery's program and especially to the presentation of significant international art. In particular, I wish to recognize Bruce Munro Wright, Chair of our Board, whose generous donation helped to realize this exhibition. I also extend my deepest appreciation to my co-curator Jeff Wall, with whom I am pleased to have worked on this, our fifth curatorial collaboration. This project and our partnership were made all the richer given the remarkable insight and nuanced perspective his participation has brought.

Finally, I extend my profound gratitude to Martin Honert for his extraordinary body of sculpture, ten examples of which are presented for Vancouver audiences to encounter "like pearls on a necklace." This phrase is one the artist himself used as he described his vision for our Gallery's presentation, but I find that it is also a fitting analogy for the exquisite self-containment and luminescent beauty of his art. It has been both a tremendous pleasure and a privilege to work with him in realizing this exhibition.

Kathleen S. Bartels, Director, Vancouver Art Gallery

INTRODUCTION

JEFF WALL

Martin Honert was born in 1953 in Bottrop, Germany, a mining town in the German Ruhr district, the country's heavy industrial centre. He is the youngest of four children. Like many artists from the region, Honert identifies with it, its proletarian character, landscape, architecture and local styles, and this has marked his work in different ways. His education and formation took place there, from a period at a boarding school as a young boy in the 1960s, to his years at the Kunstakademie in Düsseldorf where he was part of the remarkable group of artists—among them Katharina Fritsch, Thomas Schütte, Reinhard Mucha, Thomas Ruff, Rosemarie Trockel, Thomas Struth, Albert Oehlen, Andreas Gursky and Thomas Demand—who emerged there in the 1980s.

The rich traditions of modern art that had developed in the area created a multivalent situation where no single style or movement dominated; major figures like Joseph Beuys, Gerhard Richter or Georg Baselitz co-existed in a tendentious, critical, yet essentially open-minded atmosphere. Cologne and Düsseldorf were the dual capitals of this scene, but the framework of support and patronage extended throughout the area and westward into neighbouring Belgium and Holland. From the mid-1960s, art students and other young artists in the general area had unequalled direct exposure to the most innovative tendencies in contemporary art without having to follow any overriding main line of thought or attitude.

It was in this context that Honert and his colleagues began to reconsider the pre-eminence of non-figurative and anti-object art that marked the 1960s and 70s, and to find new paths to an encounter with the age-old, and possibly ageless, resources of figuration. This was not confined to the Rhineland but was an international, even global, shift of emphasis with many different manifestations.

In Germany any impulse toward figurative sculpture had to confront both the established legitimacy of the avant-garde's deconstruction of tradition and the National Socialists' sanctification of statuary in their campaign against "degenerate" modern art. After 1945 it seemed impossible to engage with any form that had been promulgated during the Third Reich. The 1950s was a time of German artists' hesitant and painful recovery of some confidence in the modern notion of figuration and in modern art generally, a part of the process of rebuilding relationships with the rest of Europe and the wider world.

The success of this process mirrored—and was part of—the "economic miracle" of the period during which Germany not only re-established itself as a European nation, but also transformed itself into a European power, commercially and culturally. The emergence of the Rhineland art scene, whose cosmopolitan outlook included an authentic appreciation for local traditions and styles, is one of the most striking examples of the postwar reinvention of German culture.

Around 1980, therefore, a new artistic and cultural confidence supported a number of independent reconsiderations of the major trends and discourses of avant-garde or neo-avant-garde art. German art in the twentieth century had been less non-figurative than any of the other European modernisms, and that identity supported a confrontation with the French-American orthodoxy of the primacy of abstraction, which stretches from Cubism to Donald Judd, Frank Stella and Richard Serra, by way of Soviet Constructivism.

Beuys was central to this development: his work confronts reductivism and minimalism, making use of aspects of them while imposing on them elements drawn from German Romanticism and Expressionism; he integrates, even appropriates, techniques, methods and styles from artists devoted to anti-literary, anti-compositional values and twists them around, making them literary and compositional once again, but without compromising the obligation to innovate formally and materially. His work sustains a longing for figuration in a period where there could be no simple return to it, regardless of the journalistic clichés of the time about the "return to painting" or the "return to the studio." Beuys' work is one of a number of imposing versions or models of an art that no longer felt obliged to take sides in the discussion about figuration and its alternatives, and as such provided an exhilarating sense of the new complexities underlying that classic duality. Sigmar Polke and Anselm Kiefer are obvious examples of Beuys' influence in the German scene of the eighties, but at the same time both Richter and Baselitz among others engaged with important aspects of the dualism outside of and even in opposition to Beuys' manner and attitudes.

Alongside painting and sculpture—the predominant forms at the time—the new developments in photography popularly identified with the "Düsseldorf School" and the teaching of Hilla and Bernd Becher were important in bringing into focus an emphasis on the objective and the everyday, an æsthetic in sharp contrast to the florid, intensely expressive character of Beuys and his protegés. Richter's "photo paintings," made from common snapshots and news photographs, and the archival works by Hans-Peter Feldmann were central reference points in this revival of the *Sachlichkeit* (Objectivity) that was an important current of the German avant-garde of the 1920s.

An objective approach to the everyday is often a mode of appreciation of the local and the specific. For Honert and others, this is part of a sometimes-passionate expression of affection for the Ruhr district. The area's concentration of mines and related heavy and dirty old-fashioned industries have left it with an unlovely but impressive landscape of modest urban centres, extensively rebuilt after the damage done to them in 1944 and 45, and factory complexes surviving from the era of European industrialization in the nineteenth century. The Bechers' photographic archive of these structures, which they have called "anonymous sculptures," is the most consistent expression of a love for the local culture of industry and of the *sachlich* spirit, which looks back to the work of the Cologne master, August Sander.

Honert's work takes this approach but applies it to a subjective starting point. In a number of published statements, he has emphasized the role that memories of his childhood play in his work. Many of his sculptures derive directly from images and documents he has retained or discovered in his or his parents' home and archives, and he has provided detailed commentaries on this source material in several catalogues.

For a catalogue entry for the sculpture *Foto [Photo]* (1993), a work in painted wood and epoxy showing a young boy (the artist age five), seated at a table covered with a patterned tablecloth, he provided a family snapshot, and added, "The model for this three-dimensional work was a slide from my parents' photo collection. The picture was taken in 1958, during a family trip to Spain … everyone in the family except me is diligently scrutinizing the maps and books spread out on the table. I am looking into the camera, because I didn't understand the game and was more interested in the black thing making a strange whirring sound—the sound of the self-timer—that was sitting on the kitchen cabinet." The slide shows Honert surrounded by his mother, father and two older brothers, but the sculpture includes only him. "I wanted to isolate this brief contact between the camera and me. The other family members, then, were no longer relevant to the realization."[1]

Photo is a meticulous recreation of the table, chair and child in the photograph. Honert has painted the piece to match both the colour range of the faded Ektachrome slide and the light and shadow pattern in the room. The surface treatment tends to excerpt the sculpture from its actual place and time in the moment of its display because it appears to be lighted by another dimension than the one in which it is being seen. This excerption mimics the way a photograph excerpts its subject from the flow of time, arrests and isolates it, and makes it into a symbol of memory.

Other subjects include birds, tents, swimming merit badges, choirboys, trees, toys, gentle mundane landscapes, as well as scenes from favourite childrens' books. Taken together, they give a sense of the emotional lives of well-brought-up children from cultured families, where books are read, responsibilities are taken seriously, tradition and religion are not scorned. There are few overt images of disobedience, anti-social behaviour, youthful rebellion or erotic adventure. A prominent sense of solitude glimmers in the overall calm, well-meaning, rational, organized, self-aware, reflective atmosphere, where reticence borders on taciturnity.

All the works are carefully crafted, their complex techniques combining modern polymer resins with carved woodwork, photographic elements, hidden lighting and transparent materials. Honert seems to seek out technical challenges. These are in part made necessary by the subject matter that attracts him—for example, *Feuer [Fire]* (1992)—but it also seems as if he needs them as ends in themselves, a condition of working and a state of mind. The sculptor's respect for the object condition of the world is expressed in the care and involvement he or she brings to the making of the object that becomes the sculpture, and Honert's work exhibits this scrupulousness in every aspect. His touch is gentle to the point of inexpressiveness and it seems as if the inexpressiveness is itself a statement about his relation to his memories. He has disclaimed any special or dramatic qualities for them, emphasizing that his childhood was not difficult or in any way traumatic, but rather dull and normal, and that, nevertheless the memories are a precious distillate of a part of his life that has vanished and can only be recalled through a meticulous effort at reconstruction and approximation.

His earliest memory images date from the later 1950s, a difficult time for the condition of memory in Germany, only a few years after the end of the war and the collapse of the National Socialist order. Remembering, forgetting, denying and accusing were activities charged with regret, shame, anger and mourning. The worried demands of the young for accounts of the catastrophe evolved into a dramatically charged conflict between the generations who lived through and participated in Nazism and their children or grandchildren who, born after the end of the war, had no awareness or connection to it but who nonetheless found themselves burdened with a profound sense of responsibility, in part through their reaction to the denials of their elders. This conflict reached its greatest intensity in the 1960s and 70s, when the international protest movements of those years triggered the violent opposition that swept through Western Germany, and which persisted well into the 1980s. That movement demanded answers from guilty parties and was vehemently convinced that punishment was required; the vehemence evoked atavistically intense reactions on the part of those whose own histories were shaped by the violence of the war years. Artists like Beuys and, following him, Kiefer, attempted to find ways to recover the dignity and legitimacy of German culture from the heap of ruin and guilt under which totalitarianism had buried it. Their confrontations with Teutonic identities were sharply if ambiguously political and they seemed to contain or admit the painful and raging feelings that the protest movements were attempting to contend with and somehow transcend.

By the middle of the 1980s more than thirty years of patient reconstruction had brought a new urban and suburban landscape into being, one that was by then beginning to look and feel quite different from what it had replaced. For thirty-year-old artists it was in this landscape that they found the elementally charged memory images of their childhoods. Their works evince a change of direction, away from rancour and painful settling of accounts, toward an encounter with the modulation of historical trauma through the sheer passage of time and the evolving viewpoint of a new population who were not able to experience history in the way that older people did, but who were in a position to begin to see with different eyes the outcome of the confrontations with the past. The calm, even bland, quality of this work was startling; it was as if it were depicting another Germany, not the familiar one, but a new one made up of recombined elements of the past and the present that had come into being without quite having been noticed. This new mood begins to appear for example, in the early photographs of Thomas Ruff, or paintings by Michel van Ofen, which depict spare, seemingly lifeless interiors of suburban houses, in Thomas Struth's *Unconscious Places*, in Hans-Peter Feldmann's books of photographs and in a number of Honert's early sculptures such as *Haus [House]* (1988), *Linde [Linden]* (1990), *Zelt [Tent]* (1991) and *Bahnhäuschen [Railway Hut]* (1992).

All these works are painstaking reconstructions of inconspicuous everyday objects, both man-made and natural. In both *House* and *Linden*, the objects are miniaturized to the scale of architectural models or possibly toys. Their uncanny accuracy and reduction in size give them a mysteriousness and gravity suggesting historical and psychological meanings that are difficult to identify. It is apparent that the artist has undergone an identification, if not with the objects themselves, then with the feeling evoked in his experiences with them, and that the objects have become romantic emblems of both personal states of being and historical or social energies that are not codified in rational forms of communication.

Where *Linden* achieves its effect through miniaturization, *Vogel [Starling]* (1992) moves in the opposite direction, enlarging the bird so that its smallest features can be examined. The relief sculpture's style derives from illustrations in bird manuals, where the sharp and fine detail must satisfy the bird watcher or researcher's need for precise identification of the different species. Like all these sculptures, the starling is isolated from any surrounding space and made to be seen as a complex and suddenly unfamiliar phenomenon, presented to the viewer without a discursive context or evident explanation. The isolation suggests an expansion of significance, as if the meanings the work discloses take possession of the void around the sculpture.

For Honert, the notion of the local is not defined by its physical characteristics alone, even though he is sensitive to them. What is local, immediate, is also that which is imagined, dreamt, read, whispered or sung about. In his commentary about *Linden* he quotes from a nineteenth century popular song about the tree's virtues. His work has an emphatic and deliberate literary dimension, and this is made most evident in the sculptures created as illustrations or embodiments of moments or scenes from children's novels or other sources. The earliest and best known of these is the *Kinderkreuzzug [Children's Crusade]*, completed in 1987. This was followed by his *Ein Szenisches Modell des Fliegenden Klassenzimmers [A Model Scenario of the Flying Classroom]* (1995), after the novel *The Flying Classroom* by Erich Kästner, published in 1933; then a set of lenticular photographs from stills from Peter Brook's 1963 film version of William Golding's famous novel *Lord of the Flies* (1954), and a second work from Kästner's novel, *Test of Courage (Flying Classroom)*, made in 1999. The premise of all these works is a treatment of children's experience of trial, conflict, adventure, friendship and the learning of hard lessons.

Children's Crusade is based on different accounts of two thirteenth century attempts by groups of children—or possibly young vagabonds—to conduct their own pilgrimages to the Holy Land in the wake of the major Crusades. These pilgrimages were apparently inspired by charismatic children and involved thousands of participants; both are said to have ended in failure and even disaster for the young crusaders, some of them reportedly having been sold into slavery somewhere near the Mediterranean. There is little definitive historiography on these events and even their existence remains speculative. Honert's version, then, is a personal projection based on his first experience of hearing about the topic at age ten. His version, not surprisingly, turns away from the more historically-likely notion of a discordant, disordered and confused movement of the impoverished and rejected, instead creating a romantic and dignified pastoral. It might be that the actual events, if they took place, were inspired by a viral religious excitement not uncommon in late medieval Europe, which could have given rise to what might be among the earliest instances of adolescent rebellion and the search for a free space outside the strictures of feudal regimes, where teens, children and outcasts could form a horde and invent their own social order, if only temporarily and under the auspices of a hallowed religious purpose. Honert treated this same theme in a distinctly dystopian way in his small work about *Lord of the Flies*, made soon after. But the *Children's Crusade* seems to face away from such a dimension; it presents the crusaders as composed and virtuous, sexually innocuous and even remote from one another, as if sincerely and impassively united only in their faith and without ulterior or subconscious motives. This apparent absence of turmoil and mixed feelings creates an eerie quality of excessive composure, as if the sculpture gestures toward erasing aspects of its subject but at the same time makes that erasure evident, even salient, and in that reversal manages to evoke the suppressed elements without permitting them to be seen. It is as if the work's subject were being read by a ten-year-old child still unaware of his or her own feelings while nevertheless being subject to them. The work installs the lack of awareness as the mark of the artist having recovered a sense of the child's mind and articulated it as that which the work cannot reveal directly, only dialectically.

The young crusaders in their chain mail and cuirasses are less individuals than they are emblems of character armour, the smoothed-out personality that is the result of repression.

Honert's interest in the armoured and inaccessible personality seems to mirror his enigmatic treatment of objects. Although he doesn't attempt to reduce beings to objects, his sculptures of human figures seem to concentrate on showing the ways in which people can appear less multi-valent and conflicted than they really are. This can extend to a satire, as in the case of the recent *Englischlehrer [English Teacher]* (2011). This polymer sculpture depicts one of Honert's school-teachers at about one-half scale and continues to show the smoothed-out simplifications of detail, texture and expression seen in many earlier pieces. The scale adjustment creates confusion about the identity and nature of the figure comparable to some of Charles Ray's works that play with the relative body sizes. The English teacher isn't small enough to be seen with the kind of affection evoked by *Linden* or *House*; he is just small enough to seem to be ridiculous, a feeling augmented by the unattractive expression on his face. The artist appears to be taking his revenge on a person from his past, breaching the decorum of his treatment of most of his figures, which is usually more detached.

The affection is striking in *Riesen [Giants]*, which can be seen as a counterpoint to the diminutive schoolmaster, and a variation on the pair of stern young knights leading the *Children's Crusade*. Once again, Honert's changes of scale create a dimensional gap and isolate the work from the audience. The two outsized wanderers seem gentle, introverted and passive, but also protective, as if they were itinerant shepherds moving from museum to gallery, watching over the crowds of art lovers, possibly shielding them from the unremembered but still echoing violence of the Gods and Titans, gigantic sculptures at the origin and heart of the Western tradition. Their highly individuated features and uncertain, complex expressions resemble those we find in the two overt self-portraits in Honert's œuvre—the child in *Photo* and the adult in *Laterne [Lantern]* (2000), as distinct from the masklike treatment of the crusaders and others. This suggests that the works in which the figures are highly individualized represent both memories and the person who is remembering, the others the memories only, the remembering person being rendered absent, masked, erased or blurred. The more individuated figures express the artist's desire for a point of view exterior to the memory itself, a position that permits the feelings and state of mind of the person subject to the memory to appear to some extent directly and independent of that memory. Other works—and these are in the majority—seem to plunge into the imaginary space of the memory itself, with the present-time psyche of the artist buried or built into that space, as if dissolved into the polymers out of which the works are made.

Lantern is the only adult self-portrait Honert has made; nevertheless, he connects it with a memory of the lanterns he carried on the Catholic St. Martin's Day celebrations. This November holiday celebrates the end of the autumn work season and marks a moment of indulgence and feasting before the beginning of Advent. Children traditionally made paper lanterns and carried them in evening processions. *Lantern* is a cube on whose four vertical faces are images illuminated with internal fluorescent lighting. Each face depicts the interior of the cube from a viewpoint perpendicular to that face. The interior is a room occupied by the artist, tucked under a cozy duvet in what might be a hospital bed, sitting up slightly and gazing at a television set placed on a wheeled cart. The television is transmitting an image of the earth seen from orbit. The room has no ceiling and the night sky, with a full moon and countless stars, spreads above a city skyline which is entirely dark save only for the glow from Martin's television.

The memory of a flimsy paper lantern has been transmuted into an object whose manufacture is remote from anything a child could make, yet we are obliged to take the artist's commentary at its word and assume that this work effects an identification of some kind with St. Martin, the artist's namesake. The work's dominant deep blue colour derives from the nocturnal atmosphere, but it may refer to the fact that blue is the liturgical colour for Advent. By identifying himself with St. Martin, Honert makes even more explicit here than in other instances the demand his works make for an iconographical analysis and interpretation, one that will involve tracing and following the transformations of identity between the source material he takes pains to keep in view and the work that is finally made.

Three other works in the exhibition—*Fire*, *Kriegslampe [War Lamp]* (2009) and the scale model version of *Schlafsaal [Dormitory]* (2013)—also feature some form of internal lighting. Honert has been intrigued with this aspect throughout his career. One of his earliest pieces, *Table with Jell-O, Red Upholstered Chair*, made in 1983 while he was still a student at the Academy in Düsseldorf, includes a replica of a chair common in his boarding school, whose upholstery is lit from within.

Fire is one of the most spectacular of these works. Honert had to create a solid polychrome form that captures the instability of flame, and he has done this with a virtuosity that reminds us of some of Gian Lorenzo Bernini's astonishing feats, as well as of the most advanced film studio trickery. Like *Linden*, *Fire* replicates a natural phenomenon by working against the inescapable fact of its inherent state of movement, giving the resulting works an uncanny arrested feeling that tends to make us experience the object as an emblem of our overall relation to nature, something we can ponder but never fully grasp or define.

Some of the illuminated pieces, like *War Lamp*, are ceiling-mounted decorated lighting fixtures devoted principally to presenting two-dimensional images. *War Lamp* is the most recent in a group of works that originates in Honert's own childhood drawings. The drawings have become the basis for sculptural groups, like *Ritterschlacht [Knights' Battle]* (2003–4), or *Nikolaus [Santa Claus]* (2002), but in the case of *War Lamp*, the images are etched into a layer on one of the lamp's two inverted domes. Lighting effects and explosions are provided by the second dome and the movement between the two domes creates the sense of a battle in progress, much the way an old-fashioned lamp with a rotating shade printed with images can conjure up movements and stories in a child's bedroom.

Honert's involvement with internal lighting has reached new levels of complication in his *Dormitory* project dating from 2010. We are presenting a one-fifth scale model version of the piece which shows the entire project, since the definitive life scale version is still incomplete. The sculpture originated with a photograph showing the dormitory of his boarding school, empty during the holidays. He decided to reconstruct in three dimensions what is seen in a photograph, as he had done on several previous occasions. But this time the reconstruction was to be of the room seen as in a colour photographic negative. The artist's commentary for this work provides no word on the reason for this decision, but it seems as if he wants to give the viewer the uncanny sense of inhabiting the imaginary interior of a sheet of photographic film. The bed, chair and wardrobe are made in acrylic material onto which has been printed the surface detail of each object, and these objects are illuminated from within, so they glow as if the negative they incarnate has been inserted into an enlarger whose lamp has been turned on. An enlarger projects the image elsewhere, usually onto a receiving surface which will transform the negative into a positive, and thereby reintroduces us to the world we normally see. The result of the completion of this transformation is what we usually call a photographic image. But in the *Dormitory* we cannot determine any direction in which the illuminated negative is being projected; it is as if the projection has been displaced to another dimension and we are suspended within the thin illuminated plane on which the colours are reversed. This plane becomes a phantom space that we find ourselves inhabiting almost against our will, like the astronaut in the penultimate scene of Stanley Kubrick's *2001: A Space Odyssey*, who, having passed through an incomprehensible dimensional warp, finds himself standing in an eerily-lit rococo bedroom, gazing at himself as an ancient creature on his own deathbed. A moment later he is reborn and, as an infant, begins his return voyage to earth. Honert's *Dormitory* is almost absurdly subdued in comparison, but not too subdued to advance its own indirect claims to having found forms for intuitions about sculpture, cinema, photography, light, dark, childhood, adulthood, memory, education, Germany, time, masculinity, loneliness and secrecy.

1 Martin Honert and Boris Groys, *Martin Honert* (New York: Matthew Marks Gallery; Cologne: Verlag der Buchhandlung Walther König, 2004).

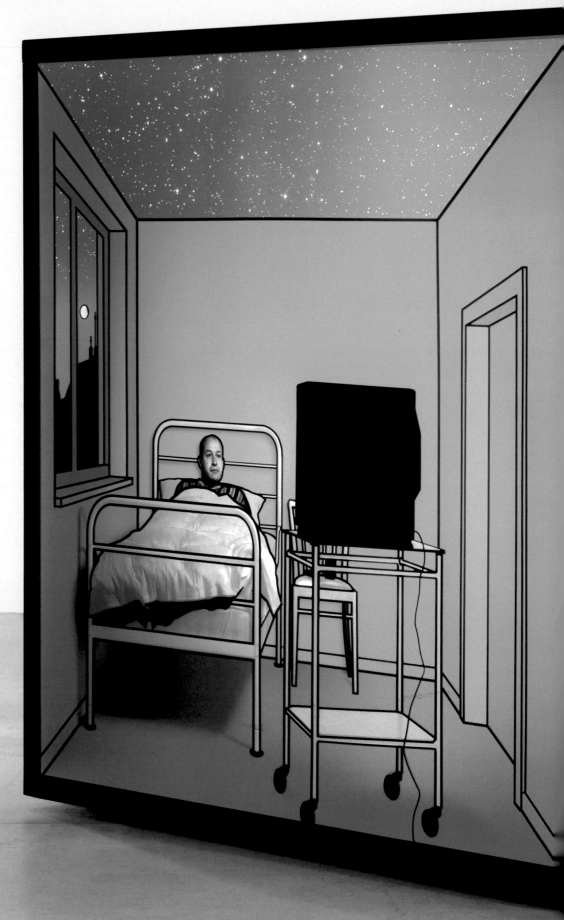

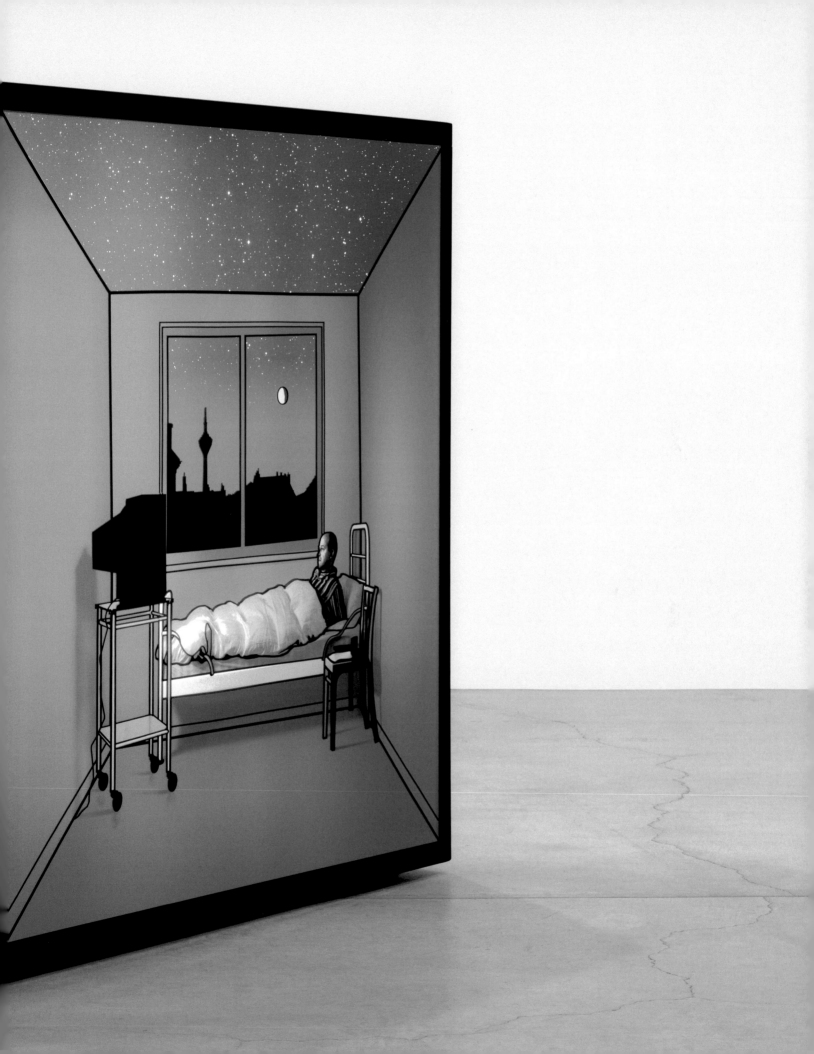

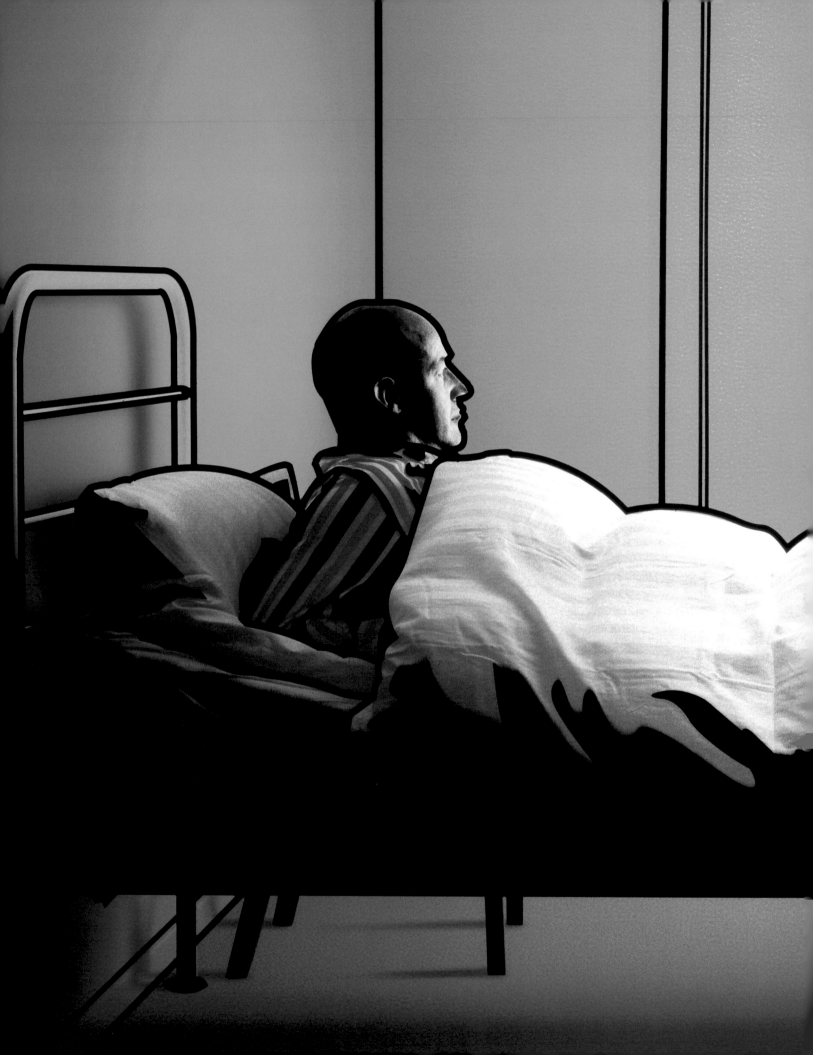

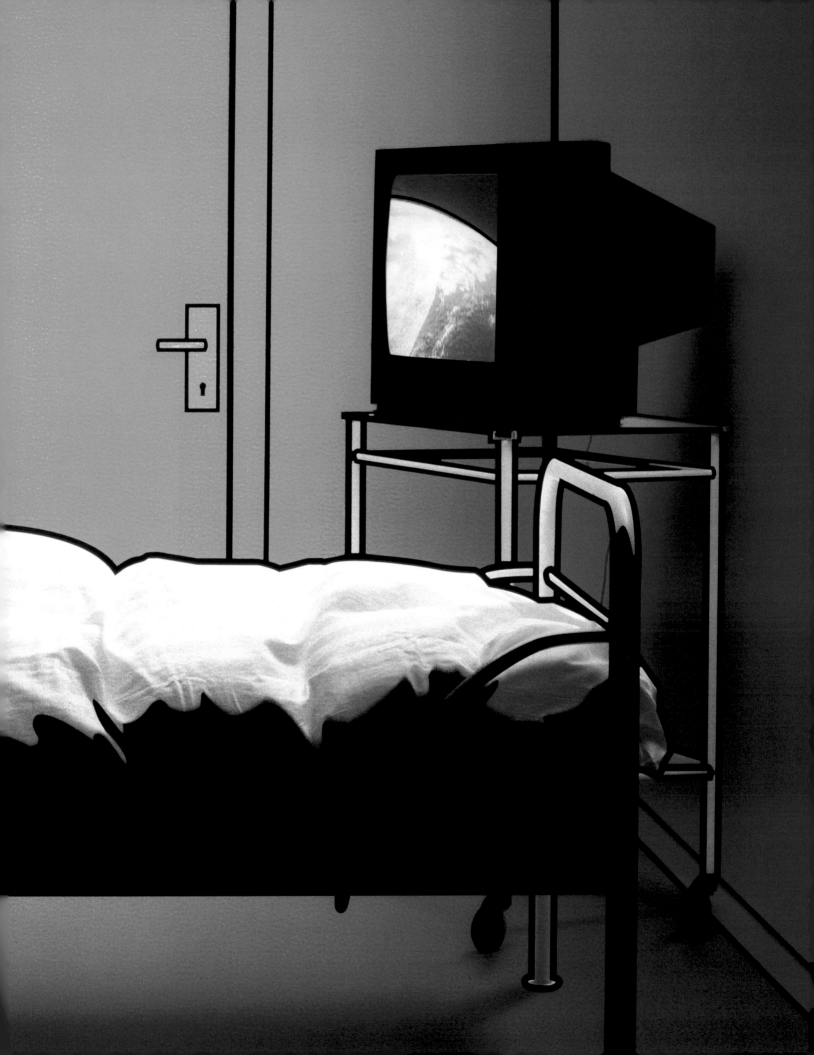

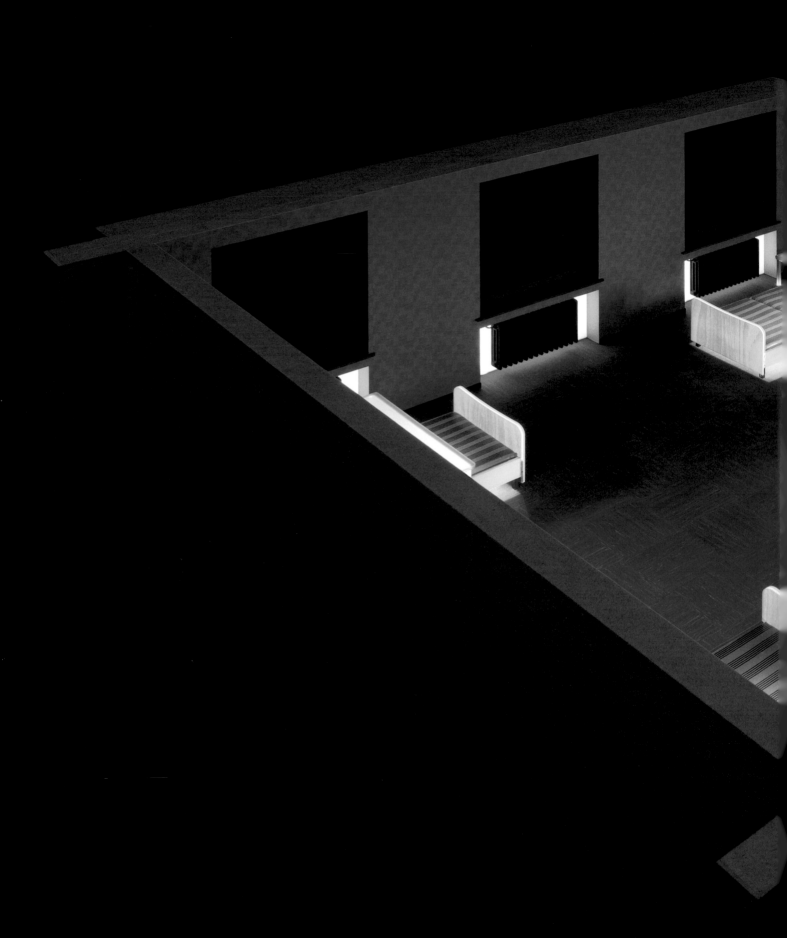

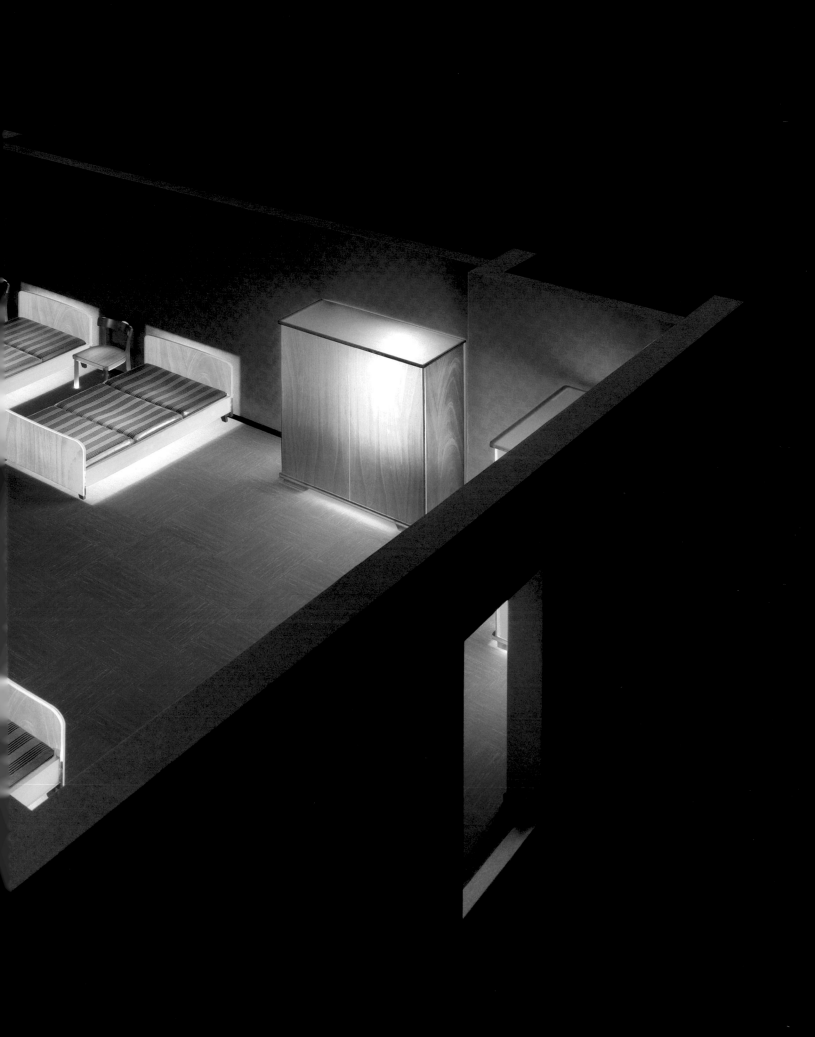

LIST OF WORKS

Kinderkreuzzug
[Children's Crusade],
1985–7
acrylic on polyester and
oil on canvas
figures: height ca. 165 cm;
relief: 200.6 x 160 cm;
canvas: 429.2 x 264 cm
Collection of Melva Bucksbaum
and Raymond Learsy

Linde [Linden], 1990
metal, synthetic foam,
plastic resin, paper, paint
edition 1 of 2
285 x 140 x 140 cm
Montreal Museum of
Fine Arts, Purchase,
Camil Tremblay Estate
and Horsley and Annie
Townsend Bequest

Feuer [Fire], 1992
painted and illuminated
polyester
201.3 x 238.9 x 198 cm
The Museum of Contemporary
Art, Los Angeles, Partial
and Promised Gift of Ivan
Moskowitz and Herbert
Moskowitz, 98.85

Vogel [Starling], 1992
polyester resin and paint
195.5 x 170 x 15 cm
Private Collection

Foto [Photo], 1993
epoxy resin, oil and acrylic
on wood
100.3 x 100.3 x 122 cm
MMK Museum für Moderne
Kunst Frankfurt am Main,

Acquired with funding from
the Margarethe and Gustav
Kober Donation, 2005/101

Laterne (Kleine Version)
[Lantern (Small Version)],
2000
aluminum, Plexiglas,
ink-jet prints, polystyrene
and flourescent lights
100 x 100 x 96.5 cm
Courtesy of Matthew
Marks Gallery

Riesen [Giants], 2007
Styrodur, polyurethane
rubber, wool, clothing, leather
300 x 100 x 80 cm
Staatliche Museen zu Berlin,
Nationalgalerie 2012
purchased by the Verein der
Freunde der Nationalgalerie

Kriegslampe [War Lamp], 2009
acrylic, foil, metal and
electrical components
73.6 x 100.3 cm
Courtesy of Matthew
Marks Gallery

Englischlehrer [English
Teacher], 2011
mixed media
150 x 50.2 x 50.2 cm
Courtesy of Matthew
Marks Gallery

Schlafsaal, Modell 1:5
[Dormitory, Model 1:5], 2013
wood, acrylic, metal, electrical
devices, ink on foil and paper
116 x 152 x 148 cm
Courtesy of Johnen Galerie,
Berlin

BIOGRAPHICAL NOTES

Martin Honert was born in Bottrop, Germany, in 1953. Since 1998 he has taught at the Hochschule für Bildende Künste in Dresden. He lives and works in Dresden and Düsseldorf.

EDUCATION

1981–1988

Staatliche Kunstakademie Düsseldorf

SELECTED SOLO EXHIBITIONS

2013

Martin Honert, Vancouver Art Gallery

2012

Martin Honert— Kinderkreuzzug, Hamburger Bahnhof—Museum für Gegenwart, Berlin

2010

Comma 21: Martin Honert, Bloomberg Space, London

2009

Martin Honert—Schlafsaal, Galerie Gebr. Lehmann, Dresden

2007

Martin Honert, anlässlich der Verleihung des Preises des Kuratoriums der Kunststoff-Industrie (on occasion of the award of the board of trustees of Plastic Industries); Kunsthalle im Lipsius-bau, Dresden; Staatliche Kunstsammlungen Dresden; Galerie Neue Meister, Dresden; and Matthew Marks Gallery, New York

2006

under cover—aus dem Verborgenen, Kunsthalle Düsseldorf

2005

Martin Honert, Landesmuseum für Kunst und Kulturgeschichte, Münster, Germany

2004

Martin Honert, Matthew Marks, New York

2002

Martin Honert, Kunstverein Hannover, Germany

2001

Martin Honert, Galerie Johnen + Schöttle, Cologne

2000

Martin Honert, Galerie Gebr. Lehmann, Dresden

1999

Martin Honert, Matthew Marks Gallery, New York

Martin Honert, Galerie Rüdiger Schöttle, Munich

1998

Martin Honert, Galerie Johnen + Schöttle, Cologne

1997

Fata Morgana [Mirage], Museu d'Art Contemporani de Barcelona

1996

Zuspiel: Martin Honert und Stefan Hoderlein, Siemens Kulturprogramm, Württembergischer Kunstverein, Stuttgart, Germany

Das fliegende Klassenzimmer, Arnolfini, Bristol, UK

1994

Martin Honert, École nationale supérieure d'art de Bourges, France

1993

Martin Honert, Galleria Massimo De Carlo, Milan

1991

Martin Honert, Galerie Rüdiger Schöttle, Munich

Martin Honert, Peter-Mertes-Stipendium (with Pia Stadtbäumer), Bonner Kunstverein, Bonn, Germany

1990

Martin Honert, Galerie Johnen + Schöttle, Cologne

1988

Martin Honert, Galerie Johnen + Schöttle (with Elke Denda), Cologne and Munich

SELECTED GROUP EXHIBITIONS

2011

Jeff Wall: The Crooked Path, BOZAR, Brussels and Centro Galego de Arte Contemporáneo, Santiago de Compostela, Spain

Dwelling, Marianne Boesky Gallery, New York

2010

The Promised Land, Albertinum, Dresden

New Work: Katharina Fritsch, Robert Gober, Nan Goldin, Andreas Gursky, Martin Honert, Charles Ray, Terry Winters, Matthew Marks Gallery, New York

2009

5 x 5 CASTELLÓ 09, Espai d'art contemporani de Castelló, Spain

2008

Vertrautes Terrain: Aktuelle Kunst in & über Deutschland, Zentrum für Kunst und Medientechnologie, Karlsruhe, Germany

Facetten der Moderne: das Menschenbild im Wandel, Skulpturensammlung Staatliche Kunstsammlungen, Dresden

2007

The Great Exhibition 2007: Royal College of Art Summer Show, Kensington Gardens and the RCA Galleries, Kensington, UK

Summer Exhibition 2007, Royal Academy of Arts, London

2006

Schöne Neue Welt, Staatliche Kunstsammlungen Dresden

The Garden Party, Deitch Projects, New York

2005

spinnwebzeit—die eBay-Vernetzung, MMK Museum für Moderne Kunst, Frankfurt am Main

Spielräume, Lehmbruck Museum, Duisburg, Germany

Film. Ist und Als-ob in der Kunst, Staatliche Kunsthalle Baden-Baden, Germany

Hot Needle (Graphic Works of the 1980s), Galerie hlavního msta Prahy/City Gallery Prague

Sammlung 2005/Collection 2005; Neupräsentation der Sammlung/New presentation of the permanent collection;

K21 Ständehaus, Kunstsammlung Nordrhein-Westfalen; Duesseldorf

2004

Die Zehn Gebote, Deutsches Hygiene-Museum Dresden

Triennale der Kleinplastik, Fellbach, Germany

2003

Animations, Kunst-Werke Institute for Contemporary Art, Berlin

Durchgehend geöffnet, Staatliche Kunsthalle Baden-Baden, Germany

2002

Kunsthaus Dresden

2001

KölnSkulptur 3, Skulpturen-park Köln, Cologne

Und keiner hinkt—22 Wege vom Schwegler wegzukommen; Museum Kurhaus Kleve, Germany; Kunsthalle Düsseldorf

2000

Human Kind, Themenhalle, EXPO 2000, Hannover, Germany

Mutprobe, Galerie Neue Meister der Staatliche Kunstsammlungen Dresden

1999

Szenenwechsel XVI, MMK Museum für Moderne Kunst, Frankfurt am Main

Unsichere Grenzen, Kunsthalle zu Kiel, Germany

Vergiß den Ball und spiel' weiter—Das Bild des Kindes in der zeitgenössischen Kunst, Kunsthalle Nürnberg, Nuremberg, Germany

1998

Szenenwechsel XII, MMK Museum für Moderne Kunst, Frankfurt am Main

1997

Drei Wege zum See, Kunstverein Klagenfurt, Germany

Szenenwechsel XI, MMK Museum für Moderne Kunst, Frankfurt am Main

Young German Artists 2, Saatchi Gallery, London

The House in the Woods, Centre for Contemporary Arts, Glasgow

1996

The book is on the table (with Tom Gidley, Siobhán Hapaska and Collier Schorr), Entwistle Gallery, London

Fondo, figura y lluvia, Galerie Antoni Estrany, Barcelona

Cabines de Bain, Piscine de La Motta, Freiburg, Czech Republic

Elke Denda, Martin Honert. Zwei Editionen, Edition Opitz-Hoffmann, Bonn

Private View: Contemporary British and German artists, The Bowes Museum, Barnard Castle, UK

Views from Abroad—European Perspectives on American Art 2, Whitney Museum of American Art, New York

En helvetes förvandling—Tysk konst fran Nordrhein Westfalen, Kulturhuset Stockholm

1995

Deutscher Pavillon (with Katharina Fritsch and Thomas Ruff), La Biennale di Venezia, Venice

Szenenwechsel V, MMK Museum für Moderne Kunst, Frankfurt am Main

Zwei und Zwanzig, Peter-Mertes-Stipendium 1985–1995, Bonner Kunstverein, Bonn, Germany

Zimmerdenkmäler, Blumenstraße, Bochum, Germany

1994

Kunsthaus Mürzzuschlag/Jahresmuseum, Mürzzuschlag, Austria

École nationale supérieure d'art de Bourges, France

Galerie Johnen + Schöttle (with Elke Denda, Stefan Hablützel, Daniel Oates), Cologne

1993

Galleria Massimo De Carlo, Milan

APERTO, La Biennale di Venezia, Venice

Menschenwelt (Interieur), Portikus, Frankfurt am Main; Castello di Rivara, Rivara and Turin, Italy; Norwich Gallery, Norfolk Institute of Art and Design, UK; Württembergischer Kunstverein Stuttgart;

Westfälischer Kunstverein
Münster, Germany

Kunstpreis der Böttcherstraße
in Bremen, Germany

1992

Double Identity, Galerie
Johnen + Schöttle, Cologne

Biennale of Sydney, Australia

Post Human, Musée d'Art
Contemporain, Pully/Lausanne,
Switzerland; Castello di
Rivara, Rivara, Italy; DESTE
Foundation for Contemporary
Art, Athens; Deichtorhallen
Hamburg

Renata Preis, Nuremberg,
Germany

Elisabeth-Schneider-Stiftung,
Freibourg im Breisgau,
Germany

*Qui, quoi, où? Un regard sur
l'art en Allemagne en 1992*,
Musée d'Art Moderne de la
Ville de Paris

MMK Museum für Moderne
Kunst, Frankfurt am Main

1991

*Art conceptuel des années 79
à aujourd'hui*, Galerie Rüdiger
Schöttle, Paris

Anni '90; Galleria Comunale
d'Arte Moderna; Bologna,
Cattolica and Rimini, Italy

1990

Carnet de Voyage, Fondation
Cartier, Jouy-en-Josas, France

1989

de Appel Arts Centre (with
Katharina Fritsch and Thomas
Ruff), Amsterdam

SELECTED
BIOBLIOGRAPHY

BOOKS AND CATALOGUES

Udo Kittelmann. *Martin Honert
—Kinderkreuzzung*. Berlin:
Verlag der Buchhandlung
Walther König, 2012.

Ulrika Groos. Georg Imdahl,
and Beate Sontgen,
*Berlinde De Bruyckere and
Martin Honert: Undercover*.
Kunsthalle Dusseldorf: Verlag
der Buchhandlung Walther
König, 2006.

Martin Honert and Boris Groys.
Martin Honert. New York:
Matthew Marks Gallery; Cologne:
Verlag der Buchhandlung
Walther König, 2004.

Boris Groys. *MARTIN HONERT:
Werkverzeichnis/Catalogue
Raisonné*. New York: Matthew
Marks Gallery; Cologne:
Verlag der Buchhandlung
Walther König, 2003.

Andreas Bee. *Zehn Jahre
Museum für Moderne Kunst
Frankfurt am Main*. Cologne:
DuMont Literatur und Kunst
Verlag, 2003.

Isabel Greschat and Matthias
Winzen. *Durchgehend
geöffnet: Skulpturensommer
in Baden-Baden*. Cologne:
DuMont, 2003.

Museum Kurhaus Kleve.
*Und keiner hinkt: 22 Wege
vom Schwegler wegzukommen*.
Kleve: Museum Kurhaus
Kleve, 2002.

Julian Heynen, ed. *Sammlung
Ackermans*. Dusseldorf: K21
Kunstsammlung Nordrhein-
Westfalen; Ostfildern: Cantz
Verlag, 2002.

Skulptur-Biennale Münsterland,
Steinfurth: Skulptur-Biennale
Münsterland, 2001.

Kunsthalle Nürnberg. *Vergiß
den Ball und spiel' weiter*.
Nuremberg: Oktagon and
Kunsthalle Nürnberg, 2000.

Dean Sobel. *Interventions: New
Art in Unconventional Spaces*.
Milwaukee: Milwaukee Art
Museum, 2000.

Jean Clair. *Cosmos: from
Romanticism to Avant-Garde*.
Montreal: Musée des beaux-
arts de Montréal and Éditions
Gallimard, 1999.

Silvia Rozenberg, ed.
*Knights of the Holy Land:
The Crusader Kingdom of
Jerusalem*. Jerusalem: The
Israel Museum, 1999.

Sammlung Lothar Schirmer.
Von Beuys bis Cindy Sherman.
Munich: Schirmer/Mosel,
1999.

Sammlung Landesbank
Baden-Württemberg. *ZOOM:
Ansichten zur deutschen
Gegenwartskunst*. Stuttgart:
Sammlung Landesbank
Baden-Württemberg, 1999.

Hans-Werner Schmidt
and Beate Ermacora, eds.
*Unsichere Grenzen: Daniele
Buetti, Bea Emsbach,
Martin Honert, Dieter Huber,
John Isaacs, Ron Mueck,*

Tony Oursler, Diego Schindler-
Castro. Bielefeld: Kerber
Verlag, 1999.

Tilman Osterwald. *Martin
Honert*. Bonn: Institut für
Auslandsbeziehungen,
Autoren and Photographen
und VG Bild-Kunst, 1998.

Scottish Arts Council.
*The House in the Woods:
Five Contemporary German
Sculptors*. Glasgow: Scottish
Arts Council, 1998.

Josephine Lanyon. *Zuspiel:
Martin Honert and Stefan
Hoderlein*. Bristol: Arnolfini,
1997.

René Block. *Pro-Lidice:
52 Künstler aus Deutschland*.
Prague: The Czech Museum
of Fine Arts, 1997.

Matthais Winzen, ed.
Zuspiel. Munich: Siemens
AG, Kulturprogramm; Bristol:
Arnolfini, 1997.

Penelope Curtis and Veit
Görner. *Private View: a
Temporary Exhibition of
Contemporary British and
German Artists*. Leeds: Henry
Moore Institute, 1996.

Dirk Lucklow and Matthias
Winzen. *Zuspiel: Stefan
Hoderlein—Martin Honert*.
Stuttgart: Wurttembergischer
Kunstverein, 1996.

Martin Honert. *Ein szenisches
Modell des "Fliegenden
Klassenzimmers" nach der
Erzählung von Erich Kästner*.
Ostfildern: Cantz, 1995.

Margarethe Jochimsen, Annelie Pohlen and Stephan Schmidt-Wulffen. *Zwei und Zwanzing: Peter Mertes Stipendium 1985–1995*. Bonn: Bonner Kunstverein, 1995.

Jean-Christophe Ammann. *Martin Honert*. Frankfurt: Museum für Modern Kunst, 1994.

Herbert Burkert et al. *Menschenwelt (Interieur)*. Munich and Stuttgart: Oktagon, 1994.

Kunsthaus Muerz, *Jahresmuseum 1994*. Mürzzuschlag: Kunsthaus Meurz, 1994.

Ulrich Bischoff et al. *Kunstpreis der Böttcherstraße in Bremen*. Bremen: Kunsthalle Bremen, 1993.

Pascal Rousseau. *Martin Honert: The Model Child*. Bourges: École nationale supérieure d'art de Bourges, 1993.

Jeffrey Deitch. *Post Human*. New York: Distributed Art Publishers, 1992.

Galerie Schneider. *Elizabeth-Schneider-Stiftung*. Freiburg: Galerie Schneider, 1992.

Musée d'Art Moderne de la Ville de Paris. *Qui, quoi, oú? Un regard sur l'art en Allemagne en 1992*. Paris: Musée d'Art Moderne de la Ville de Paris, 1992.

9th Biennale of Sydney. *The Boundary Rider*. Sydney: 9th Biennale of Sydney, 1992.

Galleria Comunale d'Arte Moderna. *Anni Novanta*. Milan: Arnoldo Mondadori Arte, 1991.

Bonner Kunstverein. *Martin Honert. Pia Stadtbäumer. Peter Mertes Stipendium 1990*. Bonn: Bonner Kunstverein, 1991.

Fondation Cartier. *Carnet de Voyages*. Jouy-en-Josas: Fondation Cartier, 1990.

Johnen + Schöttle. *Martin Honert*. Cologne: Johnen + Schöttle, 1988.

SELECTED ARTICLES

Verena Emke. "Martin Honert, Hanburger Bahnhof, Berlin bis 7 April." *Weltkunst* (February 2013): 75.

Jens Hinrichsen. "Schöner scheitern am Unmöglichen: Martin Honert, stur in Berlin." *Monopol* (December 2012): 118.

Jörg Heiser. "Schulzeit aus Resopal." *Süddeutsche Zeitung* (November 13, 2012).

Hans-Joachim Müller. "Das stille Grauen der Kinderzeit." *Die Welt* (October 27, 2012): 25.

Christiane Meixner. "Martin Honert: Wo die Reisen wohnen." *Der Tagesspiegel* (October 10, 2012).

Barbara Wiegand. "Hamburger Bahnhof: Martin Honert: Kinderkreuzzug." *Kulturradio RBB* (October 5, 2012).

"Martin Honert—Kinderkreuzzug." *KUNST magazin* (October 2012).

"Martin Honert. Kinderkreuzzug." *KQ-Daily* (October 2012).

"Martin Honert: Kinderkreuzzug." *Der Tagesspiegel* (October 2012): 9.

Brita Sachs. "Auf Tuchfühlung." *Frankfurter Allgemeine Zeitung* (June 10, 2011).

"Kunstwerk, lass uns Freunde sein." *Monopol* (March 2010): 20.

Brian Boucher. "Martin Honert." *Art in America* (February 2008): 140–41.

Ken Johnson. "Martin Honert." *The New York Times* (October 19, 2007): E35.

William Pym. "Martin Honert." *Artforum.com* (October 6, 2007).

Katya Kazakina. "German Artists' Big Bearded Hikers, Poetic Palaces: Chelsea Art." *Bloomberg.com* (October 1, 2007).

Stefan Koldehoff. "Bringt die Gaben ein." *Monopol* (October 2005): 112.

Josephine Meckseper. "Die Göttliche Linke." *Monopol* (August–September, 2005): 22–23.

David Rimanelli. "Best of 2004." *Art Forum* (December 2004): 154.

"Martin Honert." *The New Yorker* (April 19–26, 2004): 35.

Jane Harris. "Martin Honert at Matthew Marks Gallery." *Time Out New York* (April 8–15, 2004): 54.

Fernando Galán. "Drawings, What has not Gone with the Wind." *Art.es* (March–April 2004): 26–8.

Heinz-Norbert Jocks. "Und keiner hinkt: 22 Wege vom Schwegler wegzukommen." (June–July 2001): 368–71.

Saul Anton. "Martin Honert." *ime Out New York* (December 16–30, 1999): 118.

Jean Ronneau. "Unsichere Grenzen." *Kunstforum International* (September–November 1999): 375–7.

Holland Cotter. "Trans-Atlantic Mix of Parallels and Contrasts." *The New York Times* (October 18, 1996).

James Roberts. "Look and Learn." *Frieze* (March–April 1996), 52–7.

Heinz-Norbert Jocks. "Martin Honert: 'es geht um die Rettung eines Bildes, bevor dieses in mir wegstirbt.'"

Kunstforum International (August–October 1995): 280–91.

Matthias Winzen. "Martin Honert. Biennale in Venedig. Ein Gespräch." *Kunst Bulletin* (July–August 1995): 10–7.

Jean-Christophe Ammann. "Zum Beispiel: Martin Honert—Arbeit an der Errinerung." *Kunst + Unterricht* (May 1995): 10–1.

Boris Groys. "Mind's Eye Views: Boris Groys talks with Martin Honert." *Artforum* 33 (February 1995): 52–61.

Jürgen Hohmeyer. "Volkssturm in gelobte Land." *Der Speigel*, no. 18 (1995): 200–3.

Mark Pimlott. "Human World." *Frieze* (March–April 1994): 57–58.

Julian Heynen. "Martin Honert." *Artist*, no. 20 (1994): 22–25.

José Lebrero Stals. "Martin Honert: Out of the Deadpan." *Flash Art* 26 (Summer 1993): 88–90.

Olivier Zahm. "Martin Honert-Galerie Rüdiger Schöttle, Paris." *Artforum* (April 31, 1993): 105–6.

Candida Höfer. "Martin Honert-Museum für Moderne Kunst." *Flash Art* 26 (January–February 1993): 96.

Jean-Christophe Ammann. "Martin Honert." In *Bewegung im Kopf: Vom Umgang mit der Kunst*. Regensburg: Lindinger + Schmid, 1993: 236–42.

Norbert Messler. "Second Nature." *Artforum* (Summer 1992): 89–91.

Andreas Denk. "Martin Honert. Pia Stadtbäumer. Peter-Mertes-Stipendium 1990, Bonner Kunstverein."

Kunstforum International (March–April 1991): 391–2.

Norbert Messler. "Martin Honert-Johnen + Schöttle." *Artscribe* (January–February 1991): 92.

Julian Heynen. "Über junge Düsseldorfer Künstler: Martin Honert." *Das Kunstwerk* (January 1989): 143.

Robert-Jan Muller. "To be objective." *de Appel*, no. 1 (1989): 25–31.

Jutta Koether. "Martin Honert / Johnen + Schöttle." *Flash Art* (October 1988): 136.

Published in conjunction with *Martin Honert*, an exhibition organized by the Vancouver Art Gallery and presented from June 29 to October 14, 2013.

Generously supported by Bruce Munro Wright.

Publication Coordination: Kimberly Phillips and Tracy Stefanucci, Vancouver Art Gallery
Design: Mark Timmings, Timmings & Debay Design
Photography: All photographs are by Vancouver Art Gallery photographers Trevor Mills (pages 8, 30–31, 36–43, 46–49) and Rachel Topham (cover, frontispiece, pages 6, 12, 22–29, 32–35, 44–45)
Digital Image Preparation: Trevor Mills and Rachel Topham, Vancouver Art Gallery
Printed in Canada by Hemlock Printers Ltd.

Cover: *Kinderkreuzzug [Children's Crusade]*, 1985–7 (detail)
Frontispiece: *Vogel [Starling]*, 1992 and *Linde [Linden]*, 1990 (installation view)

The Vancouver Art Gallery is a not-for-profit organization supported by its members, individual donors, corporate funders, foundations, the City of Vancouver, the Province of British Columbia through the British Columbia Arts Council, and the Canada Council for the Arts.

LIBRARY AND ARCHIVES CANADA CATALOGUING IN PUBLICATION

Honert, Martin, 1953–
[Sculptures. Selections]
Martin Honert / curated by Kathleen S. Bartels and Jeff Wall.

A catalogue of an exhibition held at the Vancouver Art Gallery from June 29 to October 14, 2013.

ISBN 978-1-927656-05-1 (bound)

1. Honert, Martin, 1953– —Exhibitions. I. Bartels, Kathleen S., 1956–, writer of added commentary II. Wall, Jeff, 1946–, writer of introduction III. Vancouver Art Gallery issuing body, host

750 Hornby Street, Vancouver BC V6Z 2H7 Canada
Telephone 604 662 4700   www.vanartgallery.bc.ca